CAMEL

By Jenna Grodzicki

Consultant: Darin Collins, DVM
Director, Animal Health Programs, Woodland Park Zoo

Minneapolis, Minnesota

Credits

Cover and title page, © John Seaton Callahan/Getty; 3, © funkcanna/iStock; 4–5, © eAlisa/Shutterstock; 6, © bennymarty/iStock; © GlobalP/iStock; 7, © Priakhin Mikhail/Alamy; 8, © SimonSkafar/iStock; 9, © iStock/Oskanov; 10–11, © lkpro/Shutterstock; 12, © Ranglen/Shutterstock; 13, © Vixit/Shutterstock; 15, © Shutterstock/Pises Tungittipokai; 16–17, © Alex Tumee/Shutterstock; 18–19, © Shutterstock/Andrea Willmore; 21, © Lubo Ivanko/Shutterstock; 23, © franckreporter/iStock

President: Jen Jenson
Director of Product Development: Spencer Brinker
Senior Editor: Allison Juda
Associate Editor: Charly Haley
Designer: Colin O'Dea

Library of Congress Cataloging-in-Publication Data

Names: Grodzicki, Jenna, 1979- author.
Title: Camel / by Jenna Grodzicki ; consultant: Darin Collins, DVM, Director, Animal Health Programs, Woodland Park Zoo.
Description: Minneapolis, Minnesota : Bearport Publishing Company, [2022] | Series: Library of awesome animals | Includes bibliographical references and index.
Identifiers: LCCN 2020058661 (print) | LCCN 2020058662 (ebook) | ISBN 9781636911465 (library binding) | ISBN 9781636911540 (paperback) | ISBN 9781636911625 (ebook)
Subjects: LCSH: Camels--Juvenile literature.
Classification: LCC QL737.U54 G76 2022 (print) | LCC QL737.U54 (ebook) | DDC 599.63/62--dc23
LC record available at https://lccn.loc.gov/2020058661
LC ebook record available at https://lccn.loc.gov/2020058662

Copyright © 2022 Bearport Publishing Company. All rights reserved. No part of this publication may be reproduced in whole or in part, stored in any retrieval system, or transmitted in any form or by any means, electronic, mechanical, photocopying, recording, or otherwise, without written permission from the publisher.

For more information, write to Bearport Publishing, 5357 Penn Avenue South, Minneapolis, MN 55419. Printed in the United States of America.

Contents

Awesome Camels! 4
One Hump or Two? 6
Beat the Heat 8
Time for Dinner 10
Best Desert Friends 12
Endangered Camels 14
Have You Herd 16
A Cute Camel Calf 18
Growing Up 20

Information Station 22
Glossary 23
Index 24
Read More 24
Learn More Online 24
About the Author 24

AWESOME Camels!

CRUNCH, CRUNCH! A camel walks across the sand under the hot desert sun. With their padded feet and famous humps, camels are awesome!

A CAMEL'S WIDE, ROUNDED FEET KEEP IT FROM SINKING INTO THE SAND.

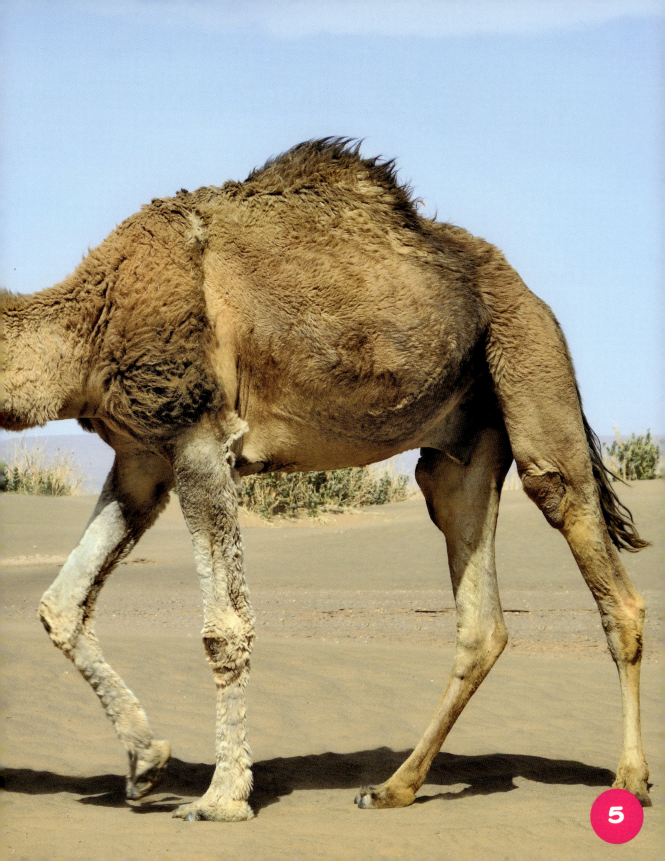

One Hump or Two?

Two kinds of camels make their way through the dry deserts of Africa and Asia. How can you tell them apart? It's easy—look at the humps! Dromedary (DROM-uh-dair-ee) camels have one hump. Bactrian (BAK-tree-uhn) camels have two humps. Camels store fat in their humps. The animals use this fat when food is hard to find.

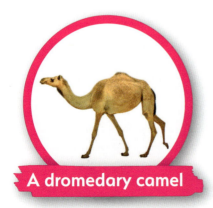
A dromedary camel

A Bactrian camel

IF A CAMEL USES ALL THE FAT INSIDE ITS HUMP, THE HUMP WILL START TO **DROOP**. WHEN THE CAMEL EATS AGAIN, THE HUMP GOES BACK TO NORMAL.

Beat the Heat

Camel humps aren't the only body parts perfect for a hot, sandy home. Three sets of eyelids and two rows of eyelashes keep sand out of camels' eyes. And that's not all! Camels can shut their **nostrils** during sandstorms.

Time to sit down? No problem! Camels have thick pads on their chests and knees to keep them from getting burned by hot sand.

Some of the deserts where camels live can get very cold during the winter. Camels grow thick fur to stay warm and then shed much of it in the spring.

Time for Dinner

These desert dwellers are mostly **herbivores**. Camels spend much of their time looking for food. And when they find something to munch on, they eat their fill. That way, there's no need to worry when food is in short supply. When they have humps full of fat, camels can go a week or more without water and several months without food.

Best Desert Friends

Camels aren't the only ones who call the desert home. Some people do, too! So, it's no wonder humans who live there have used camels for thousands of years. Camels often move people and other heavy loads across the desert. And when camels get moving, they can be pretty quick. They run as fast as racehorses! **ZOOM!**

SOME PEOPLE ALSO USE CAMEL HAIR AND LEATHER FOR CLOTHING. THEY EAT CAMEL MEAT AND MILK. SOME EVEN BURN CAMEL POOP FOR FUEL!

Endangered Camels

Camels may be helpful to humans, but humans have **domesticated** camels for so long that most of them have been taken from the wild. There are no more wild dromedary camels in their native lands. The small number of Bactrian camels that live in the wild are **endangered**. There are less than 1,000 left in the world. On top of the **threats** from humans, camels also need to be on the lookout for wolves.

Have You Herd?

In the wild, camels live in groups called herds. A herd is made up of one **male**, a small group of **females**, and their young. Sometimes males without a herd may form their own groups.

Camel herds can often be heard before they are seen! Camels **communicate** through moans, groans, bellows, and roars! They also blow in each other's faces as a way of greeting. **HELLO!**

A GROUP OF CAMELS IS ALSO CALLED A CARAVAN OR A FLOCK.

A Cute Camel Calf

The herd grows bigger when baby camels are born. Male and female camels **mate** once every two years.

Thirteen to fifteen months later, female camels will leave the herd to have their babies alone. The long-legged babies are able to walk and run almost right away, but they are missing one key camel accessory—their humps! Those won't grow for months.

Growing Up

Milk from its mother's body helps a young camel grow big and strong. A mother and her calf join the herd again after two weeks. Soon, the young camel starts to learn how to find food and communicate with other members of the herd. Most camels stay with their mothers until they are five years old. Then, they are ready to have their own babies.

MOTHERS AND THEIR CALVES HUM TO EACH OTHER.

Information Station

CAMELS ARE AWESOME!
LET'S LEARN EVEN MORE ABOUT THEM.

Kind of animal: Camels are mammals. Most mammals have fur, give birth to live young, and drink milk from their mothers as babies.

Other dessert mammals: There aren't many large mammals that live in deserts. The lack of food makes it hard for big animals. Most desert mammals are small rodents.

Size: Camels are about 7 feet (2.1 m) tall. That's about as tall as a garage door.

CAMELS AROUND THE WORLD

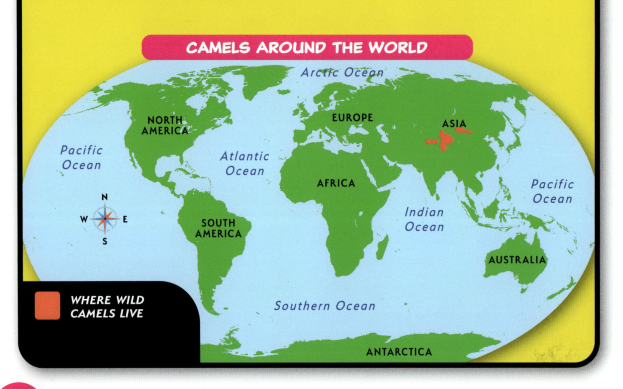

WHERE WILD CAMELS LIVE

Glossary

communicate to share information

domesticated tamed so that an animal can live with and be used by people

droop to hang down or sag

endangered in danger of dying out completely

females camels that can give birth to young

herbivores animals that eat only plants

male a camel that cannot give birth to young

mate to come together to have young

nostrils openings in the nose that are used for breathing and smelling

shed to have fur or hair fall off a body

threats things that might cause harm

Index

calf 18, 20
desert 4, 6, 9–10, 12, 22
domesticated 14
endangered 14
herbivores 10
herds 16–18, 20
hump 4, 6–8, 10, 18
mate 18
nostrils 8
sand 4, 8
shed 9
threat 14
water 10

Read More

Bloom, Cleo. *Camels (Wild and Woolly).* New York: PowerKids Press, 2018.

Topacio, Francine. *Creatures in a Hot Desert (Wild! Exploring Animal Habitats).* New York: PowerKids Press, 2020.

Learn More Online

1. Go to **www.factsurfer.com**
2. Enter "**Camel**" into the search box.
3. Click on the cover of this book to see a list of websites.

About the Author

Jenna Grodzicki lives on beautiful Cape Cod with her husband and two children. She was a teacher for a long time before she became a writer. She loves to read and go to the beach.